Nyger's Advent
JOURNEY

May your journey be blessed!
Ms. Pat Durham

Copyright © 2012 Ms. Pat Durham
All rights reserved.
ISBN: 0615901573
ISBN 13: 9780615901572

Acknowledgements

To DiAnn Mills, author, teacher, lecturer and friend, without her encouragement, Nyger's Advent Journey would never have become a reality. You are one in a million. May God continue to bless you. Keep the adventures coming!

To my friend and illustrator, Dave Bamberg, who made Nyger and his friends come to life. Thank you for your patience and your ever present smile.

To my dear Husband, Buddy Durham, for encouraging me and always believing I can accomplish far more than I can imagine. You are my best friend and husband of fifty plus years. Thank you for always cheering me on. All my love.

Table of Contents

Introduction   ix

Defining Advent   xi

Preparation for Advent Devotions:
The Advent Wreath   xiii

Devotion Time   xv

Thanksgiving Day   1

Friday, after Thanksgiving   5

Saturday after Thanksgiving   6

First Sunday in Advent   9

Nyger Finds Patrice   12

The Persimmon Tree   16

A Stomach Ache	19
Beulah Crashes the Party	21
Beulah Tells Her Story	24
A Surprise on the Pond	26
Second Sunday in Advent	29
Pastor Myer's Daughter	32
Beulah Resurfaces	35
Matilda's Baby	37
Baby Hattie	40
The Barn Animals Share	42
Warm Beds for Everyone	45
The Third Sunday in Advent	47
Hunter is Discovered	50
The Animals Care for the Dog	52
Hunter is Well Enough to Go Outside	54
Hunter Explores the Garden	56

Table of Contents

Hunter Meets Allene	58
Hunter and Allene Become Very Good Friends	61
Fourth Sunday in Advent	65
Hunter Tells Allene's Story	67
Patrice and I Begin to Realize Our Purpose	69
Candy, Nuts, Fruits and a Christmas Tree	71
The Families Decorate the Christmas Tree and More	73
The Animals Get Ready for Christmas	76
Christmas Eve	78
About the Author	83

Introduction

Nyger's Advent Journey is an inspirational and entertaining Advent Children's Devotional Book. It begins with Thanksgiving Day and ends with Christmas Eve.

Nyger, the main character, is a big brown field rat. He has a square face with jaws that look like he is storing up nuts for the winter. His little head is bald on top because he was caught in a grass fire. He takes refuge in the little clap board church on the hill. Nyger is joined by Patrice, a white circus rat who has spent her entire life in a cage until Nyger frees her. Beulah, the bat, has lost her radar and can no longer hunt at night for nectar. Hunter, the big Labrador retriever, has an accident and must be nursed back to health by Nyger and Patrice.

All the action takes place around the turn of the twentieth century in the small white clap board church that sits on the hill in the country. Each character has a challenge or a need that can be met by one or more of the other characters. They learn to depend on each other and on their Creator God. Simple lessons are taught that the youngest child can understand. There are deeper lessons that can be grasped by the older children and still more complex lessons that only the adults may understand. During the week of Christmas, Nyger, Patrice, Hunter and Beulah learn the purpose that they have for their lives that extends beyond the little church. The devotional book targets children ages three years through the third grade.

Defining Advent

The term "Advent" comes from the Latin *Adventus*, meaning coming or appearance. Advent is the season marking the four Sundays before Christmas and developed as a way of helping Christians prepare not only to celebrate the birth of Jesus Christ in his First Coming but also to help them look forward to his glorious Second Coming as the "King of Kings and Lord of Lords."

Many Advent traditions come from Germany. Martin Luther, the great reformer, used the traditions to teach the families, including the children, of the coming of Jesus Christ.

One of the best known is the Advent wreath. The wreath itself represents the never ending love of God. The green of the wreath represents the hope of eternal life and the four candles represent the four weeks in Advent. Each week begins with Sunday.

The first candle represents the Hope that the message Christmas brings us as we recall the birth of the promised King. The second candle represents God's love that He shared in the person of his

Son. The third candle is the candle of joy. This candle is traditionally pink because it is represents the excitement that we feel that Christmas is so very near. The fourth and last Advent candle is the candle of Peace. On Christmas Eve, Christians around the world switch to all white candles signifying the birth of the Christ Child.

An Advent Calendar can also be used. Each day has a Christian Symbol that can be used to teach the truths of Jesus Christ and His mission here on earth. The Advent Calendar can be a fun and educational activity for the whole family.

The following devotions were written with busy families in mind. Each day's devotion is well within 15 minutes.

Preparation for Advent Devotions: The Advent Wreath

1. Purchase or make wreath with four taper-sized candle holders.
2. Purchase four taper candles: three purple and one pink.
3. Decorate according to your individual style and taste.
4. Place the four candles in the candle holders to be lit each Sunday in Advent.
5. Place the wreath where it is the center of your devotional time.
6. Put a lighter or matches and a candle snuffer near in readiness.

Note: You may replace the four candles with white taper candles for Christmas Day or put one large white candle in the center of the wreath for the twelve days of Christmas.

Suggestion: Be sure to protect the surface of the table against wax spills.

Devotion Time

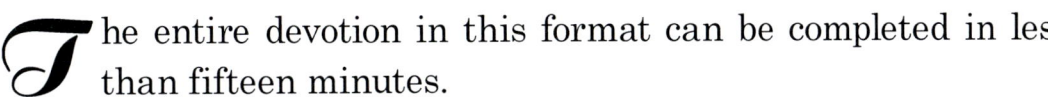

The entire devotion in this format can be completed in less than fifteen minutes.

1. Gather the family.
2. Assign a "special" family member to light the candle(s) and tell about the significance of the candle for that week. *(See Defining Advent)*
3. Sing a Christmas Carol. It doesn't have to be a sacred carol. Use the song as a teachable moment.
4. Read the scripture for the day.
5. Read the devotional message.
6. Place the ornament for the day on the Christmas tree.
7. Ask for prayer request. Pray.
8. Sing another Christmas Carol and go forth in joy!

Suggestion: Have the children and adults take turns leading the devotional time. The amount of time depends on individual families.

Thanksgiving Day

I am Nyger, a farm rat, and I have an exciting story to share with you. It was Thanksgiving Day and I had just finished a delicious breakfast of corn and grain. As I was leaving the Schroeder's barn and skipping across the pasture, out of nowhere a fox pounced on me. I jumped straight up in the air and started running as fast as I could. He was gaining on me when a huge black dog started to chase the fox. The fox forgot all about me and took off with the big dog racing after him.

My knees where shaking and my teeth were chattering I could hardly breathe. After a few minutes, I pulled myself together and cautiously made my way to the little clapboard church on the hill.

Nyger's Advent Journey

I had just curled up in a nice clump of grass in the field next to the little church. It had been a great harvest. My tummy was round and my cheeks looked like I was storing up nuts for the winter. Being a farm rat is a great life. There are lots of good things to eat and places to run and play. I play hide and go seek with my brothers and sisters every chance I get.

Thanksgiving Day

As usual, the farm families came to church in their wagons, buggies and some on horseback. They had come to give thanks to God for the wonderful harvest. I heard them singing "Now thank we all our God with hearts and hands and voices." It sounded great! I joined in and sang along with them. After the service was over, the great big wooden doors opened and the people came out of the church and visited with each other. I could hear the men talking about their barns being full of corn and hay. All of the farm animals would have plenty to eat this winter. Those full barns meant I would eat well all winter, too. The mothers were telling stories about all the fruits, vegetables and sweet jams and jellies they had canned.

The boys and girls were my favorite! After sitting for a long time, they needed to run and play. They were chasing each other everywhere. The families said their good byes and got back into their wagons and buggies or mounted their horses for the ride home. They were all planning to have a Thanksgiving Feast.

After all the earlier excitement, the warm sun, the soft grasses and gentle breezes lulled me to sleep. I dreamed of all the good things God had given me, especially the big black dog.

Let every creature praise his holy name for ever and ever. Psalm 145:21 (NIV)

Thank you, dear Father, for all our blessings. Amen.

I awoke with a start! I heard the church bells ringing and farmers shouting excitedly to each other. They were calling to start the water brigade. Smoke rose all around me and I had a hard time breathing! I couldn't see which way to go. I ran back and forth! The farmers beat the burning grass with wet sacks and blankets. I dove into a gopher's hole to escape from the fire!

Friday, after Thanksgiving

The brave men battled the flames for a very long time. At last the fire was out! Everything grew quiet. I crept out the hole. The smell from the fire stung my nostrils, my eyes were watering and the hot ground burned my feet. It was dark outside. The farmers joined in a prayer of thanksgiving. No one had been badly injured and the church had been kept safe. I waited until everything was silent, and I made my way to the little church.

Someone had left the wooden door cracked open just enough for me to squeeze inside. The little church gave me a feeling of safety. I thanked God for His protection and in spite of my burns; I curled up in a ball and went to sleep.

Your steadfast love O Lord, extends to the heavens…..people and animals you save, O Lord. Psalm 36: 5-6 (ESV)

Thank you for protecting Mommy and Daddy and all those that I love!

Saturday after Thanksgiving

I was stiff all over and my feet hurt. I slowly moved into the morning sunshine streaming through the stained glass window by the altar and warmed my back. I smelled like smoke, and my head and whiskers were singed by the flames. I opened my eyes to see and everything was blurred. I blinked several times, but my eyes must have been hurt by the fire. I started to panic. How would I find my way if I could not see?

Saturday after Thanksgiving

The light from the window was very bright. It made little rainbows all around me. Suddenly, one of the little rainbows reflected off something that was lying on the floor right in front of me. It was a pair of glasses. I slowly placed them on my nose.

"I can see! I can see," I cried.

One of the humans who had come to church on Thanksgiving Day must have left his glasses. How very fortunate for me. Being able to see again gave me hope, and I was very grateful. I bowed my head. "Thank you, dear God for keeping me safe and helping me to see again."

The righteous cry out and the Lord hears them; He delivers them from all their troubles. Psalm 34: 17 (NIV)

Thank you for our health, home and family. Amen.

First Sunday in Advent

The next day I felt much better. While I was explored all the great places to hide in the little church, I heard a great commotion! The humans were back!

I ran for a place to hide and I hopped onto one of the pews. A lady with a funny hat with feathers sticking out everywhere almost sat on me. I jumped down and scampered under the pew. A farmer wearing great big boots almost stepped on me. I quickly ran up the stairs to the safety of the balcony. I peeked out through the balcony railing to see what was going on below.

I saw people everywhere: big people, little people, and more ladies with hats and men with bushy mustaches. I heard someone call the man standing up front, "Pastor Myer." I chucked in spite of my fright. "What a funny name," I said.

    I can tell you one thing, these humans loved to sing! They were singing about Emmanuel. Pastor Myer thanked God for sending Emmanuel, Jesus, Savior of the world. I knew about the God that created me but who was "Jesus?"

First Sunday in Advent

Pastor Myer said to the congregation, "Light one candle in your Advent Wreath each day this week when you and your family have your Advent Devotions just as we did this morning in church." Pastor Myer prayed, "God bless Your children and keep them safe until we meet again next Sunday."

That sure made me happy to know the humans would be back. I wanted to know more about Jesus. Everyone started to leave the church and I decided it was a good idea to stay just where I was away from any boots!

The church became very quiet and I could feel a Sunday afternoon nap coming on.

She will give birth to a son, and you are to give him the name, Jesus...Matthew 1:21 (NIV)

Thank you, Father, for the gift of your son. Amen.

Nyger Finds Patrice

After a great night's sleep I woke up raring to go. The morning sun was coming in through the stained glass window making little rainbows everywhere! Boy, I wanted to go outside and enjoy just being alive. I felt so good my front paw started tapping and I couldn't help myself. I just started to dance. I danced all through the little church and out the front door. The morning was cool and crisp but the sun shone warm and bright. I danced this way and that and around until I was too dizzy to stand up. I fell to the ground and let out a big, Yee Haw! I was mighty grateful to be alive.

I heard a low rumble and the ground started to shake. I looked down the road and saw a big cloud of dust appearing on the horizon. It came closer and closer. A big wagon drawn by six huge horses sped towards me. I didn't waste any time running for cover.

The wagon came around the bend right in front of the little church going lickity split. Something fell off the back of the wagon and bounced to a stop right in front of me. My heart thumped so hard that I thought it would burst from my chest. After the dust cleared, I opened my eyes, squinted, and peeked out from behind a clump of dried grass.

I don't mind telling you that right in front of me was the most beautiful creature I had ever seen! It was white, and when it opened its eyes I could see they were blue just like the sky. The creature peered at me through something with bars all around it. I had never seen anything like this. I gathered up all my courage and sniffed the creature. The little white furry creature sniffed back. "Hello," It said. I jumped straight up in the air! When my knees stopped trembling, I studied the creature. "Hello, and who are you?" "I am Patrice, a white circus rat," she said. "Who are you? "Why I'm Nyger, the brown farm rat." "Where am I?" She said. "You are at my home" I said.

Just about that time, I remembered my manners and, I asked Patrice to come inside the church. Patrice could not get out of the cage. I used my sharp front teeth to gnaw through them and freed her. She took a very timid step out of the cage. I could tell she was a little scared. She ran around and around the cage. The wind was blowing on her little face, and I could she see she was filled with joy. As I watched, something must have gotten into my eyes because they started to water. Ok, I admit it. Those were tears of joy for my new friend, Patrice!

As she started to walk with me into the church, she froze. Freedom was scary. I reached out my hand to her. "Just take my hand and I will protect you," I said. "Don't be afraid. You are with me." She took my hand and we went into the safety of the little white church on the hill.

And now this word to all of you: You should be like one big happy family, full of sympathy toward each other, loving one another with tender hearts and humble minds. 1 Peter 3: 8 (TLB)

Father, help us to show love and compassion to those we meet today. Amen

The Persimmon Tree

The morning was bright and beautiful with little frosty crystals forming on the windows. This was a perfect morning to raid the persimmon tree in Pastor Myer's garden.

"Come on Patrice," I said. "Let's go get some juicy persimmons for breakfast."

"What is a persimmon?" Patrice said.

"You have never had a persimmon?" I asked.

"I didn't have persimmons in the circus."

"You are in for a treat." I said. I rushed out to the garden. I looked back and Patrice was not there. I quickly turned back to find her.

Patrice was hiding under a bench.

"What is wrong?" I asked.

"I... I... I'm afraid." Patrice said.

"I am sorry I left without you." "Please don't be afraid." I took Patrice's hand and we walked slowly to the garden.

The Persimmon Tree

As soon as we reached the garden, I climbed the tree to select a perfect persimmon. I inched out on the limb to select a prize one. "Please be careful." I don't want you to fall," Patrice said.

"Don't worry about me," I said.

The tree branch was not as strong as I thought. My weight made the limb dip and it almost threw me to the ground. "Nyger, please be careful." Patrice screamed. I turned around and ran back towards the trunk of the tree. The prized persimmon firmly grasped in my mouth. I shimmed down the tree and dropped the persimmon at Patrice's feet.

"Oh, Nyger, you are so brave."

I admitted I was frightened but I wanted to give her the best persimmon on the tree.

Patrice smiled sweetly. "Thank you." "You are a very dear friend."

Continue your love to those who know you, your righteousness to the upright in heart. Psalm 36:10

Thank you, Father God, for my friends and brothers and sisters. I am so glad I have those who love me and I can in turn love them.

A Stomach Ache

"Oh," I groaned. "I should not have eaten those last three persimmons." "Is there anything I can do for you?" Patrice asked. "No, I will just have to wait until my stomach stops hurting." I didn't want to worry Patrice. "My mother always told me not to be a piggy. Hee hee. I just couldn't help myself." It seemed like a good idea to eat one more persimmon. But now I am sorry that I ate too much.

"Nyger, thank you for helping me be brave." I enjoyed being in the garden. There were so many interesting things to do and see. The birds were singing and flying from tree to tree. The squirrels were busy burying the acorns and pecans. "Nyger, will they remember next spring where they buried the acorns and pecans?" "Yes, they'll remember where they buried the nuts and be able to dig them up for a quick meal," I said. "Our Creator God gave the squirrels, you and me a keen sense of smell that helps us find our food."

"The bees are amazing creatures. They make honey for everyone to enjoy," I said.

"The world is such a beautiful and wonderful place," Patrice replied. "We must remember to thank God every day for His beautiful world."

"Thank you, Patrice for reminding me to always be thankful," I said. "God rescued me from the fire. He made a way for me to see again, provided a safe place for me to live and brought you to be my friend."

"Nyger," Patrice said. "I have so much to be thankful for, too. God allowed me to be free from the cage. He brought me to you and this little church and now He is having you help me to be brave."

We bowed our heads and gave thanks right where we were.

My heart leaps for joy and I will give thanks to him in song. Psalm 28:7 (NIV)

Thank you Father for the beauty of your world; from the tiniest or creatures like the bees to the huge whales in the ocean. Amen.

Beulah Crashes the Party

While a storm raged outside the little white church, Patrice and I explored some of the nooks and crannies of the balcony. A sound like someone scratching on the bell tower wall surprised us.

Patrice turned to me, "What can be making that sound?"

"Maybe the wind is blowing the sleet against the wall," I said. Something whirled by our heads and banged into the balcony rail. We ducked just in time! It whirled by again. Bang! It slammed into the balcony wall and dropped to the floor. Patrice was so frightened.

"Stay close to me," I said. I didn't want Patrice to know I was afraid, too. I stuck my head out and tried to look brave. "Who is it?"

All I heard was the rain beating on the roof.

"Who is it?" I repeated.

"It's Beulah, a high squeaky voice said. 'Where am I?"

"You are in the little white church," I said.

"What happened to you?" Patrice asked.

"I'd been out with my brothers and sisters gathering nectar when the storm came." Beulah said.

"Are you hurt?" Patrice said timidly.

Beulah sighed and patted her wings, "No, I don't think so."

"You are welcome to spend the night," said Patrice. "Thank you, I would like that," Beulah said.

I felt blessed to offer the shelter of the little church to someone who was in need.

Dear friends, let us practice loving each other, for loves comes from God and those who are loving and kind show that they are the children of God. 1 John 4: 7 (TLB)

Thank you that each day our love grows for you Father and for others. Amen.

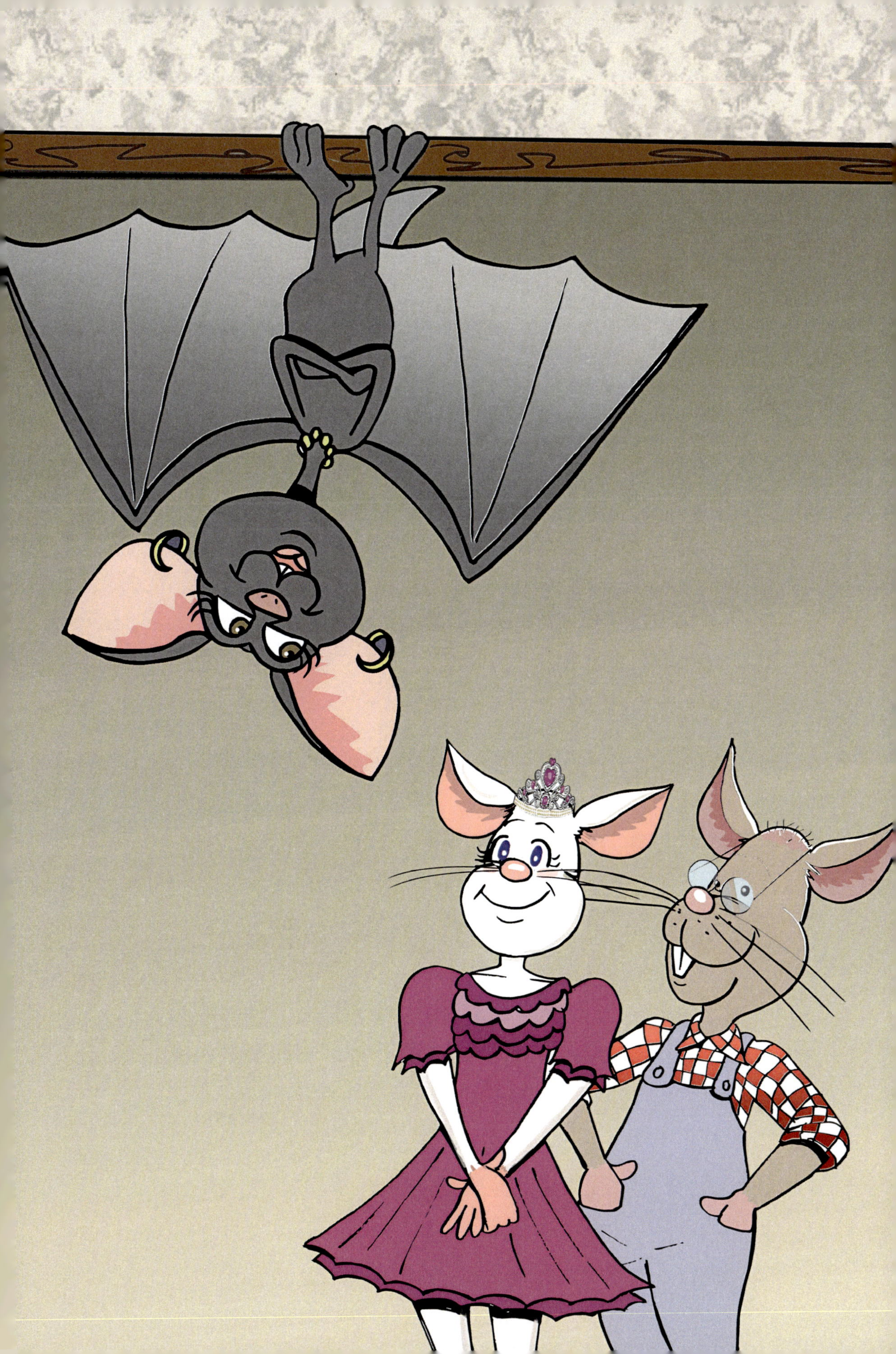

Beulah Tells Her Story

What a sight to behold! The next morning Patrice and I stared in amazement at the little black creature that had swooped down on us the night before. There she was hanging upside down from the seat of the church bench.

"What is a Beulah?" Patrice whispered.

We looked at each other and shrugged. We didn't know. Beulah stretched her little wings and opened her eyes. We must have frightened her because she let out a squeal that made my ears ring. Patrice scurried behind me.

"Good morning", Beulah squeaked. "What is wrong with you, haven't you ever seen a bat sleep before?"

We both shook our heads, "No." Well, that explained what a Beulah was. It was a bat!!! We could not help but laugh at ourselves.

Beulah told us that bats have something called radar. It helps them to see where they are going when they are out flying at night. "Bats don't go out during the day," she said. "They sleep during the day; hanging upside down," like we had seen her doing earlier.

Beulah told us that she had been having trouble with her radar. It just wasn't working like it should. The high winds and lightening had made it difficult for her to keep up with her brothers and sisters. That was why she had flown into the little church the night before.

We told her she was welcome to stay with us. "Thank you for a safe place." Beulah started to sniffle. She took one of her little wings to wipe away a tear. Beulah closed her eyes and began to sway softly back and forth. I know she was praying. Patrice and I tipped-toed away as quietly as possible.

When Jesus spoke again to the people, he said, "I am the light of the world, whoever follows me will never walk in darkness, but will have the light of life". John 8: 12 (NIV)

Dear Father, thank you for the Bible that shows us the way to Jesus. Amen.

A Surprise on the Pond

"Patrice, let's go to the pond and see what the ducks and geese are doing." I said.

"That sounds like fun." Patrice said. "Will it be dangerous?"

"No." I said, "It will be fun. We can watch the ducks and geese. When they dive into the water to catch their food, they turn upside down. All you can see are their feet and their little tails. They just bob upright and swim along just like nothing happened."

"Nyger, do they really do that?"

"Of course they do." I said.

We ran down the hill to the pond. Patrice was enjoying herself. She passed me and hid in a clump of tall grasses and jumped out at me. I was happy to see her enjoying her freedom.

A Surprise on the Pond

When we reached the pond, we saw a wonderful sight. A mother duck had her new fluffy yellow babies on their first outing. She quacked her encouragement to her six new babies.

We watched from a distance so we would not frighten the new ducklings. Patrice whispered, "Nyger, see how the babies follow their mother?"

"They stay close to her." I replied. "She makes sure they are safe from any danger."

When the ducklings had finished their first swimming lesson, the mother led them out of the water onto the shore. She showed them bugs that were good to eat. Each baby in turn had their lunch. When the swimming and eating lessons were over, the mother duck gathered the ducklings around her. She protected them under her wings. It was time for their afternoon nap.

Patrice and I quietly made our way back to our home. When we were safely inside, we discussed how our Heavenly Father invites us, His creatures to come to Him for protection. He will never turn us away.

He will cover you with His feathers, and under His wings you will find safety. Psalm 91:4

Heavenly Father, I feel your loving arms around me. You watch over me when my mom and dad can't be there. Amen.

Second Sunday in Advent

I awoke with my tummy letting me know it was time for breakfast. I made my way to Pastor Myer's barn for a tasty ear of corn. Just as I started to eat, I remembered that Patrice would need breakfast, too. Before I ate another bite, I grabbed that delicious ear of corn and ran back to the church.

Patrice was very grateful for breakfast. She thanked me and gave me a great big smile!

Suddenly, I could hear noises coming from outside. The humans were coming back to the church! It must be Sunday morning! "Quick!" I said. "Run to the balcony." The humans are back for church.

Nyger's Advent Journey

All the humans sat in pews and Pastor Myer welcomed them. I noticed that two of the candles had been lit in what Pastor Myer called an Advent Wreath. He said that the second candle was the candle of love. Then I remembered that last Sunday's candle was the candle of hope.

"What does Advent mean?" Patrice whispered.

Pastor Myer raised his hand before I could answer. "Advent is a time to prepare our hearts for the birthday of Jesus." Pastor Myer said.

Pastor Myer talked to the humans about Jesus, God's Son, who was born in a manger a very long time ago. "Jesus is the Hope for the world," he said. The people sang "Come into my heart Lord Jesus. There is room in my heart for you." The way they sang those words made me want to sing, too.

After Pastor Myer said words of blessing, everyone left the church with big smiles on their faces. They were filled with hope and love.

May the God of hope fill you with all joy and peace as you trust in him, so that you may overflow with the hope by the power of the Holy Spirit. Romans 15: 13 (NIV)

Thank you dear God that we have joy and peace in our lives. Amen.

Pastor Myer's Daughter

Monday morning we all slept later than usual. The excitement of church had made us tired. We were relieved that Beulah slept through the service. We had a feeling she would not have been very welcome.

"Her flying around and bumping into things would have been disruptive," Patrice said. "I could see Beulah getting all tangled up in one of the lady's strange hats or even worse one of the farmer's big bushy mustaches." I said. The thought of this made us both chuckle!

I talked at great length about yesterday's church service. I noticed that Patrice was very quiet. I asked her if anything was wrong.

"Did you notice the little human on the front bench who was sitting all alone?" She said. I agreed that I had.

She seemed sad and didn't walk like the other humans?"

Again, I agreed that I had noticed.

"She left the church after everyone else had gone," Patrice said,

"Pastor Myer carried her and she had a strange looking thing attached to her leg." I said.

"What do you think that means?" asked Patrice.

All but the tiniest of humans walked. This little girl was bigger. It was a mystery. In time we would know the whole story.

He will take great delight in you, he will quiet you with his love, he will rejoice over you with singing. Zephaniah 3: 17 (NIV)

Thank you Father that you love us so much you sing at the very thought of us. Amen.

Beulah Resurfaces

I stretched and yawned. The sun shone through the stained glass window providing warmth and making beautiful rainbows all over the floor of the little church. What a great way to start the day.

Patrice was all snuggled up with her cute little pink nose tucked under her front paw.

Peace and quiet ended quickly. Swish! Bang! Screech! Bong! Kaplop! Beulah flew into one of the kerosene lamps that hung from the ceiling of the church. Not only was her radar out of whack, but she had her days and nights all mixed up. Poor Beulah! When she saw the little rainbows, she thought it was night time and those were the stars.

When Beulah got all worked up, she had a hard time calming down. When she cried, Patrice stepped out from under the bench and spoke softly to her. Patrice was so gentle and thoughtful. Beulah calmed down and peace was again restored. Before we knew it, she was hanging from the underside of the church bench sound asleep with her little wings tucked around her, body swaying gently and snoring loudly.

Grace and peace be yours in abundance through the knowledge of God and of Jesus Christ. 2 Peter 1: 2 (NIV)

Thank you gracious Father that you give to us, your children, your peace. Amen.

Matilda's Baby

What a perfect day! We had gone to the meadow behind the church to play in the gopher and rabbit holes. I sure have missed my brothers and sisters, but having Patrice to run and play with helped me not be sad. When the sun set, a full moon and stars lit up the night.

I had just drifted off to sleep dreaming about the delicious persimmons and pecans that had fallen from the trees and all the delicious corn that was in Pastor Myer's barn.

Beulah swooped down screeching at the top of her lungs. Wake up! Wake up! Patrice jumped so high she hit her head on the bench. My glasses flew across the floor.

"Matilda the cow has had a baby calf and it is a girl". "The sheep, the horse, the ducks, the geese and hens are so excited. Mother and baby are doing well. You have to come and see. Follow me!'"

Patrice and I waited at the door while Beulah re-oriented herself to make her way to the barn. It took quite a few tries before she finally got through the door and headed in the direction of the barn. She circled around the bell tower several times before she got it right.

There in the moon light was Matilda with her new baby by her side. All the animals were gathered around. No one said a word. The only sound that could be heard was the cooing of a mama and papa dove up in the rafters of the barn. The sight brought tears to my eyes.

And God said, "Let the earth bring forth every kind of animal- cattle and reptiles of every kind."....And God was pleased with what he had done. Genesis 1:24 (TLB)

Dear God, thank you for my pet(s). Amen.

Baby Hattie

I am no expert on babies but I don't believe a more beautiful baby calf had ever been born. The little calf was black as the night with a beautiful little white heart on her forehead. Her nose was pink. Her hair was all wavy and the very tip of her tail was white. Her legs were wobbly.

Matilda, her mother, was a very handsome black cow with white spots. She mooed softly at us. "Have you come to see my baby, Hattie?"

"Yes, she is so beautiful." Patrice said. "Thank you," Matilda said.

Sam, the sheep, Dobbin, the horse, and all the other animals gathered around like family. The beautiful brown and white hens settled in their nest and clucked amongst themselves. Matilda groomed little Hattie by gently licking her beautiful black silky coat. Hattie was soon soundly asleep on the sweet fresh hay of the barn. She was tuckered out. We tiptoed out of the stable and made our way back to the little church.

Patrice and I were quiet. I thought about the miracle that had just happened. Patrice reminded us of Pastor Myer's words on Sunday. "All things bright and beautiful; all creatures great and small; the Lord God made them all."

Then God looked over all that he had made, and it was excellent in every way. Genesis 1: 31 (TLB)

Dear God, thank you that everything you make is good. Amen.

The Barn Animals Share

A norther blew in during the night bringing with it more sleet and ice. The cold wind whistled around the steep bell tower. The next morning we shared the warn sunbeams with one another. Patrice was concerned about little Hattie. I knew she would not be at ease about that new baby calf until she could see for herself that everything was ok.

We braced ourselves and lowered our heads against the cold blast of air. We could hardly get our breath as we ran to the barn. Matilda along with Sam, the sheep and Dobbin the horse, had made a fine wind break for the new calf. Little Hattie was enjoying a wonderful breakfast of warm milk from her mother.

Pastor Myer had already been out to the barn to feed the animals. Sam and Dobbin were munching on some new hay, the hens were in their warm nests laying eggs for the Myer family and the ducks and geese had just returned from an early morning swim on the pond. There was a lot of quacking and honking.

When Sam saw that Patrice was shivering from the cold, he offered her some of his nice soft wool to help keep her warm.

"Thank you for your kindness," she said.

"Baaa, be warm and come back soon."

We told everyone goodbye and ran quickly back to our warm home.

Continue to love each other with true brotherly love.
Hebrews 13: 1 (TLB)

Thank you, Father that my family loves me and I love them. Amen

Patrice and I used our sharp teeth to pull the wool apart and make a wonderful bed. We decided the best place was behind the altar. The sunbeams came in through the window in the early morning and warmed the spot. Perfect!

Warm Beds for Everyone

We had explored the little church thoroughly except the organ. It was scary. On Sunday mornings it startled us. However, Patrice and I were curious about the strange wooden box that didn't make a sound unless a human was sitting in front of it. We walked cautiously around it. We sniffed. It was not that scary after all.

I found a hole to crawl into the box. "Patrice, follow me," I said.

"I...I don't think so Nyger. It looks dark in there," Patrice whispered.

"It will be fine." I said.

We heard footsteps coming into the church. They came closer and closer. Patrice had scampered out of sight under the front bench.

"Nyger run!" She screamed.

I couldn't move. I could see the human's boots right outside the hole. Air swished by my whiskers. Then it happened! The loud noise started. Just like on Sunday mornings.

After what seemed an eternity, the swishing and the noise stopped. The human stepped away from the box and started for the door. I had my eyes closed and my hands over my ears.

"Nyger, are you alright?" Patrice said.

My ears rang and my knees knocked. "I think so."

"I was worried about you."

"I don't think I will be exploring the organ again," I said. "Once was enough."

Patrice gently patted my shoulder and said, "Nyger, sometimes I think you are too brave."

Make music to the Lord with the harp, with the harp and the sound of singing, with trumpets…shout for joy before the Lord, the King. Psalm 98:4 (NIV)

Father, sometimes I am so happy I just can't help but sing. Thank you for the gift of music. Amen.

The Third Sunday in Advent

Sunday started out with Beulah giving us an update on Matilda and Hattie.

Pastor Myer had fed the animals early this morning. Beulah overheard him remark to Matilda that he was going to let her and Hattie have an afternoon run in the pasture. This made Matilda very happy. Little calves have lots of energy! Just like little humans.

Patrice and I made a quick run to the barn to gather some corn for our breakfast. She out ran me. It was wonderful to see Patrice not be afraid.

The animals were catching up on the day's gossip.

"It is Sunday morning and Pastor Myer was earlier than usual with breakfast for us". Dobbin the horse said.

"He is happiest on Sunday than or any other day of the week". Sam the sheep said.

"He loves to sing and this morning he was singing, "O, Little Town of Bethlehem." Matilda the cow said.

After our breakfast, we noticed Pastor Myer and his daughter making their way to the church. We heard him call her, Allene. She wore warm mittens, boots and a brown fur hat. He carried her tenderly.

Patrice and I watched until they disappeared into the church and then we quietly entered and scooted up the stairs to peek through the balcony railing. Allene was on the front bench.

The Third Sunday in Advent

The church started to fill up with humans. We both hoped Beulah stayed asleep. Pastor Myer stood up to welcome everyone. He lit the third candle on the wreath. That candle was called the candle of joy and it was pink just like Patrice's nose! It wasn't blue like the others. Pastor Myer said it was a different color to remind everyone it was almost Christmas and this should fill everyone with great joy! It sure filled all of us with joy.

Pastor Myer invited everyone to join in singing, "O Come all ye Faithful." The organ played louder than usual as everyone sang with all their hearts. Pastor Myer's big bass voice sounded like thunder. I couldn't help but wonder if that was the way God's voice sounded.

Rejoice in the Lord always. I will say it again: Rejoice! Philippians 4: 4 (NIV)

Dear Father, thank you for the joy that you give to us through Jesus Christ our Lord and Savior. Amen.

Hunter is Discovered

So many exciting things had happened this week. Little Hattie was born and the next day we had church. It was a great service. We are all getting excited about Christmas. Not too sure what Christmas will look like when it gets here, but the humans sure are excited. That made us excited!

Patrice and I have made several trips to the barn today. She just can't get enough of seeing Hattie. That little calf kicks up her heels and sticks her tail straight in the air and around and around she runs in the corral. She just gives everyone joy.

It is getting late now. The sun is starting to set. The sky is filled with beautiful watermelon and persimmon colors and everything is still. You can hear a cows mooing and dogs barking from the farms around the little church.

Patrice and I gathered in the little church to get ready for the night. Suddenly, we hear a very sad sound coming from the outside of the church.

Patrice startled, "It sounds like someone is hurt!" "Nyger, please see what is making that terrible sound," Patrice said. I stepped to the door and tugged as hard as I could to open it. What a terrifying

Hunter is Discovered

sight! Something big and black was on the outside of the door, and it was moaning! I jumped back inside!

"What is it?" Patrice asked.

"I am not sure," I said. "But it is huge."

By this time Patrice had poked her head around the door to get a better look. Suddenly Beulah whizzed by and circled the big black object. "It's a dog." She said. "And it must be hurt."

Patrice and I pulled the poor creature inside the church. We could see he had been in some kind of accident. We helped clean the wound and bandage it. After a short time, the dog fell asleep and so did Patrice and I but Beulah was off to tell the barnyard animals about our latest adventure.

He answered: "'Love the Lord your God with all your heart and with all your soul and with all your strength and" with all your mind'; and, 'Love your neighbor as yourself.'" Luke 10: 27 (NIV)

Dear Father, thank you that because You first loved us, we are able to love and care for others and their needs. Amen.

The Animals Care for the Dog

During the first night the dog came to us, Patrice kept watch over him.

"Patrice, I believe this is the very dog that saved my life when the fox was chasing me and trying to have me for breakfast." I said.

"Then we must do everything we can to repay his kindness." She said.

As soon as the sun came up, Patrice was off to the barnyard to ask Sam for more wool. He happily shared some of his soft coat.

He had more than enough. She told Matilda, Sam and Dobbin that this injured dog once saved me.

"He is a noble creature and we must all do whatever we can to help him." Dobbin said. Everyone nodded their heads in agreement.

Beulah had been to the barn during the night and had filled in the exciting details of our evening to all the animals. Matilda offered some of her warm milk.

Patrice and I made trips back and forth to the barn to bring the wool and milk. Patrice made a bed for the dog so that he would be more comfortable. He seemed grateful for everything we were doing for him.

After such an exciting evening, Beulah slept hanging upside down from her favorite bench. She swayed back and forth with her little wings tucked around her body.

I told Patrice about the big black dog that had rescued me from the fox. "I wonder if this could be the same dog" I said. "He sure looks the same." "Nyger, said Patrice, isn't it wonderful that God has given us the opportunity to return the kindness?" Patrice always knew the right thing to say.

"A new commandment I give you: Love one another. As I have loved you, so you must love one another." John 13:34 (NIV)

Dear Father, thank you for grandparents, aunts and uncles who love us and help take care of us. Amen.

Hunter is Well Enough to Go Outside

Patrice and I took turns keeping an eye on the dog. He was feeling much better this morning. "What is your name?" I said to him.

"Hunter" he replied, "I am a Labrador retriever."

The sun was shining through the beautiful windows, and it warmed Hunter. It made him feel like getting up and stretching.

Hunter looked at us and said, "Thank you for taking care of me."

"You are welcome." Patrice replied.

"I think I will go outside." Hunter said.

"We will go with you," Patrice said.

"I'd like that." Hunter said. "It will be good to have your company." Hunter's front right leg was bandaged and he walked with a limp. Other than that he seemed to be just fine.

Even with a wounded leg it was hard to keep up with Hunter. Little Allene was sitting by the window of her house, and I saw her see Hunter just about the time that Hunter saw her. I had a feeling that this was going to be the beginning of a friendship.

"You didn't choose me! I chose you! I appointed you to go and produce lovely fruit always, so that no matter what you ask for from the Father, using my name, he will give it to you." John 15: 16 (TLB)

Dear Father, please help us always to use our gifts and talents to your glory and to help our friends and family. Amen.

Hunter Explores the Garden

Hunter stretched and yawned. He was feeling much better this morning. Everyone had a great night's sleep. After so much excitement, it was good to have some quiet time.

Hunter started out to the garden to walk around. He was stiff and his leg was still sore. It felt good to move around.

I watched Hunter as he was walking in the garden. There was Pastor Myer on his way to the barn with a basket in his hand. I was not sure how Hunter would react to Pastor Myer or the other way around. I just froze and held my breath.

Pastor Myer stopped and said, "Hello there big fellow." "I don't think I have ever seen you before. It looks like you've been hurt." As he knelt down, Hunter walked slowly over to Pastor Myer and lowered his head so that he could have his ears scratched.

Pastor Myer chuckled. "Why I do believe you've found a home if you want it."

Hunter let out a big happy bark. I think that was a yes!

Hunter followed Pastor Myer to the barn. It was time to gather the eggs. Hunter watched as Pastor Myer reached carefully under the big beautiful hens to remove the eggs that they'd just laid. When the egg gathering was completed, Pastor Myer invited

Hunter to come to the house with him. Hunter wagged his tail and smiled the biggest smile I believe I have ever seen! He gave Pastor Myer's hand a big lick and trotted along beside him to the steps, up on to the porch, through the door and into the house. As the door closed behind them, I hurried back into the little church to tell Patrice the good news!

"I have told you all this so that you will have peace of heart and mind. Here on earth you will have many trials and sorrows; but cheer up, for I have overcome the world." John 16: 33 (TLB)

Thank you Jesus that you know all about our problems and help us to solve them. Amen.

Hunter Meets Allene

Patrice and I were very curious about Hunter and his new home. He had not come back to the little church last night. We all hoped that was good news.

The sun was just beginning to pour in through the windows when Beulah swooped through the door and circled the room before she came in for a landing. She had news about Hunter, and we were anxious to hear.

"Good news", she shrieked. "The animals in the barn yard told me that Hunter and Pastor Myer came to feed them last night. Matilda was concerned about Hunter and Hattie. There was no need to worry. All is well!"

With that, Beulah was in her usual spot sound asleep. She had completed her mission.

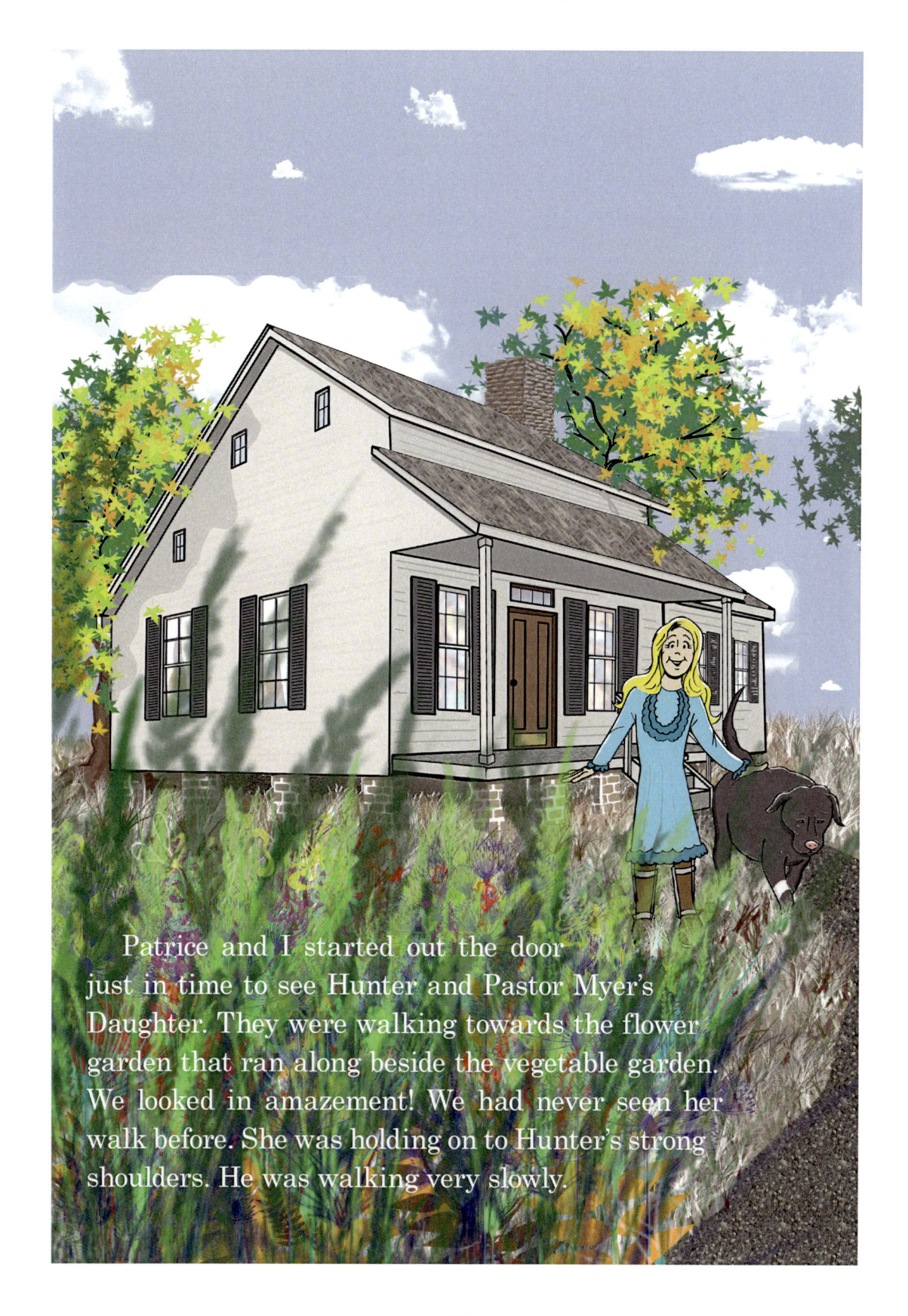

Patrice and I started out the door just in time to see Hunter and Pastor Myer's Daughter. They were walking towards the flower garden that ran along beside the vegetable garden. We looked in amazement! We had never seen her walk before. She was holding on to Hunter's strong shoulders. He was walking very slowly.

Pastor Myer called to his daughter, "Allene, please be careful and do not go too far."

"Yes, Papa, I will be careful. Allene said. Hunter is taking good care of me. I am fine." Hunter's tail began to wag and his smile got bigger and bigger.

Patrice turned to me and smiled sweetly. "I believe Hunter has found a home."

"I will not leave you as orphans; I will come to you." John 14: 18 (NIV)

Dear God, thank you for providing a wonderful home for us to enjoy. Amen.

Hunter and Allene Become Very Good Friends

Night had come and the kerosene lamp was shining brightly in Allene's window. Patrice and I scampered up onto the porch to get a better look inside. What we saw warmed our hearts. Allene was sitting in her bed with pillows propped up behind her and a feather comforter pulled up to her waist.

"I'm waiting for Papa to come and read me a bedtime story," she said to Hunter.

Hunter was lying beside her with his chin resting on her knee. Allene stroked his beautiful black coat. "You are the best Christmas Gift I could ever hope for." With each stroke of her little hand, Hunter's tail would do a roundabout and flop. We could see his eyes closing with contentment.

Hunter and Allene Become Very Good Friends

Patrice and I watched as Pastor Myer read Allene her bedtime story. He gave her a kiss and prayed with her. He prayed, "Dear Father, thank You for this day and the special blessing of having Hunter in our lives. Please protect and keep us this night and always. Amen." He carefully blew out the lamp and told Allene good night. Then he gave Hunter a final pat on his head and gently closed the door.

After one final peek, Patrice and I made our way back to the little church. Our hearts were filled with gratitude.

Don't just pretend that you love others: really love them. Romans 12: 9 (TLB)

Please take care of all the animals that do not have homes. Provide them with food and shelter until someone adopts them. Amen.

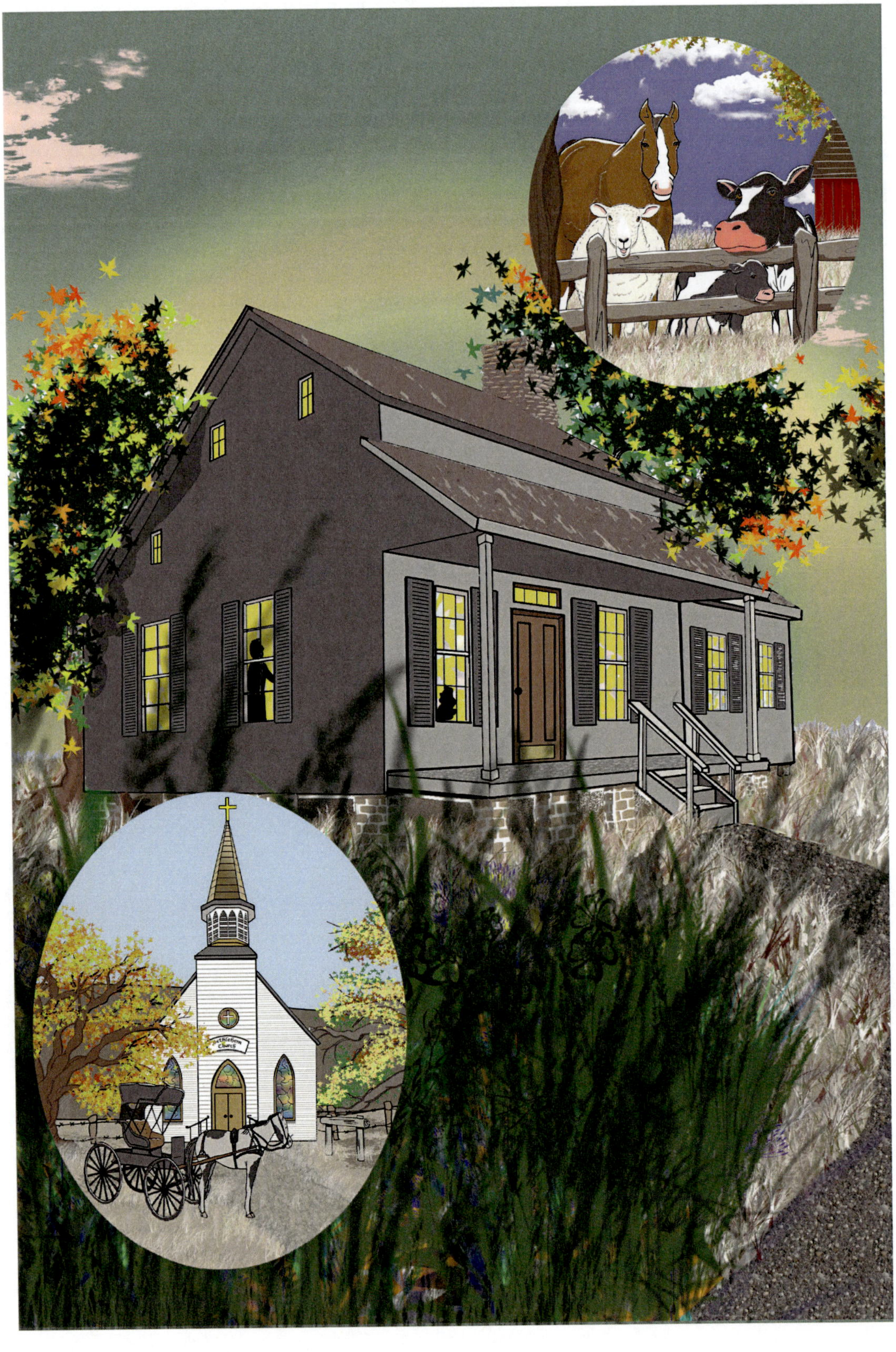

Fourth Sunday in Advent

The day dawned with the most beautiful sunrise I believe I have ever seen. The colors were shades of pinks, corals and vivid orange. Patrice and I scurried out to see the barnyard animals and grab a quick breakfast of tasty corn.

We said good morning to Hattie, Matilda, Sam and Dobbin. Matilda reminded us it was Sunday. We knew the humans would be back.

"Nyger, we must hurry back to the little church and go up stars to the balcony before everyone starts to arrive," Patrice said.

We got upstairs just in time to see something that made us take notice. Pastor Myer walked into the church without Allene. "Where could she be?" I asked.

Just about that time we saw Hunter and Allene walking up the center aisle right to the front bench. Allene took her seat, and Hunter lay down on the floor beside her. Pastor Myer was beaming from ear to ear! He helped her with her coat and mittens.

The humans seemed more joyful than usual this morning. The boys didn't squirm as much. Neither did they kick the back of the benches. The little girls sat with their hands folded in their laps and their little ankles crossed. The mothers and fathers were more polite and thoughtful of each other.

Pastor Myer lit the fourth candle and proclaimed it was the Fourth Sunday in Advent and this candle was called the candle of peace. He told the humans about the Baby Jesus who came from heaven to be born in a lowly stable. He reminded them that Jesus is the Son of God, the promised Messiah, Savior of the world. At the end of the service, a special prayer of thanksgiving was offered for Allene.

Everyone sang "Hark the Herald Angels Sing," Pastor Myer proclaimed a blessing on all the humans. After the final hymn was sung, everyone came to the front of the church to give a hug and kiss to Allene. Hunter sat right by Allene and received many friendly pats on his handsome head.

For unto us a Child is born; unto us a Son is given; and the government shall be upon his shoulder. These will be his royal titles: "Wonderful," "Counselor," "The Mighty God," "The Everlasting Father," "The Prince of Peace." Isaiah 9: 6 (TLB)

Lord Jesus, you left your royal home in heaven to come to earth to be our Savior. Thank you. Amen.

Hunter Tells Allene's Story

Patrice and I awoke with the warm sun streaming in through the windows. It was going to be a clear crisp day with just a little nip in the air.

Beulah had already zoomed in and was sound asleep. We heard the big wooden door creak and a rush of cold air followed by the paddity, pad, pad of Hunter's feet.

"Good morning," Hunter said.

"Good morning," we responded. Patrice and I started to talk at once. We wanted to know all about Allene.

"We must be quiet so that Hunter can tell us," Patrice said.

Hunter told us about Allene's accident. "She and her father had been visiting one of the farm families. They were on their way home when their buggy's wheel hit a huge hole in the road, and Allene was thrown out of the buggy. Her leg was broken in several places. She was very discouraged because it left her with a limp. When she saw me walking with a limp, she was encouraged. So, we are a good team. Pastor Myer says I have found my purpose. I know I love Allene and her father. It makes me happy to be helpful."

Then Patrice, being wiser than me clapped her hands. "That is wonderful! You will make a perfect companion for Allene. We are happy for you."

"Yes," I replied. "We are very happy for you."

Forget the former things; do not dwell on the past. See, I am doing a new thing!" Isaiah 43: 18-19 (NIV)

Thank you that we are able to do acts of kindness for our parents, brothers and sisters. Amen.

Patrice and I Begin to Realize Our Purpose

Last night Patrice and I talked about how happy we were for Hunter. It was a perfect fit for Hunter and the Myers. Hunter needed a loving home. Allene needed someone to encourage her. And all Pastor Myer needed or wanted was to see his little girl happy. Hunter was not only a good companion for Allene, but he was also a good companion for Pastor Myer. Hunter was right there at Pastor Myer's heels when he fed and cared for the animals in the barnyard. They took long walks in the meadow in the warm afternoon sun.

Beulah flew into the room. "Let me tell you what happened last night!" She screeched. "A fox was trying to snatch one of the hens for his dinner when I sounded the alarm. Donner gave him a swift kick and sent him on his way without dinner."

"Oh my, Patrice said. "Is everyone all right?"

"Yes," Beulah said. "Now I must return to the barnyard to make sure everyone stays safe."

Patrice and I knew that Beulah had found her purpose, as well. She was needed to protect the barnyard animals. She would be able to drink the nectar from the flowers in the garden and there were plenty of those pesky mosquitoes in and around the garden and barnyard to provide food for her.

Patrice turned her sweet face to me, "Nyger, what is our purpose?"

I couldn't answer that question for her right then, but we were about to find out!

Most important of all, continue to show deep love for each other, for love makes up for many of your faults. Cheerfully share your home with those who need a meal or a place to stay for the night. 1 Peter 4: 8-9 (TLB)

Thank you for our warm beds, delicious meals and our soft cuddly toys. Amen.

Candy, Nuts, Fruits and a Christmas Tree

The morning had dawned bright and clear! There seemed to be magic in the air. Patrice and I had slept well. We were thanking God for his protection throughout the night and bringing us to such an awesome morning.

Beulah had come in a little while ago after standing watch throughout the night in the barnyard. She was quite tired and had gone straight to her favorite bench to have a long nap.

Hunter had helped Pastor Myer with the morning chores, and, that all was well with the barnyard animals after the scare with the fox. They told us how brave Beulah had been and how much the animals appreciated her.

Suddenly our conversation was cut short by wagons pulling up to the front of the church. We could hear the humans talking excitedly and some were even singing! We made a dash for the balcony! The door opened wide and in came the humans pushing and pulling a huge cedar tree! They took the tree to the front of the church and stood it up on the right. It almost touched the ceiling.

The humans congratulated themselves on finding such a beautiful tree for the church.

The farmers' wives started to bring out boxes of shiny things. Some of the shiny objects were like balls. Others were long and looked like beautiful vines. Several very long ladders were brought into the church. The farmers positioned them around the tree. They brought in boxes from their wagons that smelled wonderful.

They told each other they would be back later to decorate the tree and fill gift bags for all the children. We couldn't wait for them to leave so we could explore all the new things!

"I am leaving you with a gift-peace of mind and heart! And the peace I give isn't fragile like the peace the world gives. So don't be troubled or afraid." John 14: 27 (TLB)

Thank you that we never have to be afraid because you are with us. Amen.

The Families Decorate the Christmas Tree and More

As soon as the humans had gone, Patrice and I hurried down the stairs. The cedar, apples, oranges, pecans and peppermint candies all smelled wonderful.

We were planning to raid the apples and peppermint candies but did not have time because we could hear the humans starting to return to their job of decorating the Christmas tree.

Patrice and I settled under one of the benches so we could watch.

For the rest of the afternoon, the humans from the smallest child to the largest farmer helped to decorate the tree. It was beautiful. The glittery balls and something the humans called garlands were hung and draped all over the tree. Patrice noticed with a lot of interest tiny white candles being placed all over the tree. The humans ate cookies and drank hot chocolate and apple cider all the while singing Christmas Carols.

The Families Decorate the Christmas Tree and More

The last item to be placed on the tree was a golden star. One of the farmers held a small child up over his head so he could put the star at the very top of the tree. When there were no more decorations to drape or hang, the humans put a bucket of water and another bucket of sand by the tree.

Small brown paper bags were neatly lined up under the tree. One apple, orange, several pecans, and peppermint candy was placed in each bag. Everyone stood back to admire their work. One of the mothers proclaimed it to be the most beautiful tree ever and everyone gave a big Amen! They were all singing "God Rest Ye Merry Gentlemen" as they climbed aboard their wagons and buggies to head home.

That night some shepherds were in the fields outside the village, guarding their flocks of sheep. Suddenly an angel appeared among them, and landscape shone bright with the glory of the Lord... Luke 2: 8-9 (TLB)

Thank you for showing your glory to the humble shepherds. Amen.

The Animals Get Ready for Christmas

We were all so excited for Christmas that we had a hard time settling down for the night. Beulah had awakened from her long nap and became disoriented with a huge tree right there in front of her. Patrice helped her calm down. We told her about the humans bringing the tree and then decorating it.

"I am so sorry I missed all the excitement," she screeched.

Patrice and I were mighty pleased she had slept through it. Humans and bats just don't mix.

Patrice couldn't sleep, so we ran to the barnyard to visit with the animals there. They were more peaceful than usual.

"Tomorrow is Christmas Eve," Matilda said. "Pastor Myer and Hunter were here earlier to make sure there were extra corn, hay, and even some apples for Dobbin on Christmas Eve."

"Yes, on Christmas Eve I get extra apples, Dobbin said. 'Pastor Myer says he wants me to know how much he appreciates me. It's my job to see that he and Allene get to wherever they need to go."

"Yes, Dobbin sometimes has to wait outside in the cold for hours while Pastor Myer visits with the sick and with parents who have had a new baby," Matilda added.

Each of the animals in turn told us what they did for the Myer Family. The animals were well taken care of, and they loved Allene and her Papa.

The peace that the barnyard animals felt rubbed off on Patrice and me. We were ready to go back to the church and curl up in our beds for the night. When we reached our home, we prayed a prayer of thanksgiving for all the blessings that God had provided for us and for our friends in the barnyard.

They were badly frightened, but the angel reassured them. "Don't be afraid," he said. "I bring you the most joyful news ever announced, and it is for everyone!" Luke 2: 10 (TLB)

Lord Jesus you came for everyone. Thank you that you did not come just for the rich and powerful but for everyone everywhere. Amen.

Christmas Eve

When Patrice and I awoke, we noticed that Beulah had not come back to the little church last night. We knew she had found her purpose and was probably sound asleep after watching out for the safety of the barnyard animals.

Hunter came by to let us know that the humans would be coming to church today before it was dark. This would be a special service to celebrate Jesus' birth. We were getting so excited.

Patrice and I had talked well into the night about what Beulah and Hunter had said was our purpose. They told us we had shown love to them. They had talked it over with the barnyard animals and it had been decided that Patrice and I should come and live in the nice warm barn with the animals. We would be close to everyone. Each was in agreement that our purpose was to show love.

We took the wool that Sam the sheep had given us and took it to the barn. There in the very back corner where it was warm we made our beds. This would be our new home. But first we would go back to the little church and enjoy with the humans the wonderful Christmas Eve Service.

Just as the sun was setting, the wagons and buggies started to arrive. All the humans were bundled up against the chill in the air. The lanterns helped them to make their way into the little church. Someone had lit all the little candles on the Christmas tree. It looked like hundreds of twinkly stars. The buckets of water and sand were just a precaution in case of fire.

All the candles in the Advent Wreath were lit. Something called a crèche was on the floor under the Christmas tree. Pastor Myer welcomed everyone and all the little children came up front and told the story of Jesus' birth. Pastor Myer read the account from Luke 2:1-20. All the humans joined the children in singing carols. At the end of the service, everyone was given a candle, after it was lit, everyone sang "Silent Night, Holy Night".

Nyger's Advent Journey

When they had finished singing, each of the children was given one of the bags that were under the tree. Everyone wished each other a "Merry Christmas" and hurried off to their homes because very dark clouds were approaching announcing a blue norther was coming quickly and they must reach their homes before it arrived.

80

Christmas Eve

The room was silent. All the candles had been extinguished. Patrice and I tiptoed to the crèche and knelled before the Christ Child. We were so humbled to be in his presence. We looked around us. All was well. We walked through the big wooden door and left it open just a crack. Patrice and I ran quickly to the sturdy barn as the icy winds slammed into us and snuggled down into the sweet fresh hay. With grateful hearts, we wished each other a Very Merry Christmas and fell soundly asleep.

Today in the town of David a Savior has been born to you; he is Christ the Lord. This will be a sign to you: You will find a baby wrapped in strips of cloth and lying in a manger. Luke 2: 11-12 (NIV)

Lord Jesus we want to join with children and adults all over the world in wishing you a "Happy Birthday!" Amen.

About the Author

Pat Durham, Professional Coach and CEO of Diversity-Unlimited Institute of Etiquette and Protocol, has been in business for twenty one years. Her mission statement is to redefine today's business men and women to meet the challenges in tomorrow's competitive global market place. During the past twenty one years, Pat has been a presenter at workshops, conferences, seminars, and as a key note speaker throughout Texas.

When Pat was 12 years old, she wrote an essay chronically her imaginary journey down the Amazon River. She was awarded with an A+ for her effort. That sparked a love affair with words.

The following year, she entered an essay contest sponsored by the Roy Rogers and Dale Evans Show aired on WOAI, San Antonio, Texas radio station. She wrote a short essay entitled, "What it means to be an American. Pat was awarded an appearance on Roy and Dale's radio show.

In 1957, Pat was chosen to enter her essay entitled, "What it means to be a Christian," in the Concordia University's Field Day Event. It was a three minute extemporaneous presentation before a panel of judges.

During Pat's high school years, the Lower Colorado River Electric Corporation sponsored an essay and personal interview contest. Pat was chosen as an alternate delegate to the then Senator, Lyndon Johnson, in Washington, D.C.

More recently, Pat created and implemented The Events of Advent a devotional booklet for Resurrection Lutheran Church.

Pat has served in the Ministry to Youth. Areas of service were puppetry, clown, chancel dramas, art and music. All scripts were written by Pat.

Pat's love of working with youth extend to the children that she works with at local public and private schools and the summer Life Skill classes. All materials used are compiled by Pat.

In 1996, Pat began her statewide ministry with the Lutheran Women's Missionary League. She traveled statewide conducting conferences and speaking at conventions. In 1998, Pat was honored with the nomination of Lutheran Woman of the Year. In 1999, Pat wrote an article for the Lutheran Witness.

The Federation of Houston Professional Women honored Pat with the "Woman of Excellence Award."

Made in the USA
San Bernardino, CA
22 September 2015